phen Kendrick is a speaker, screenwriter, and producer whose film
ts include *Facing the Giants, Fireproof, Courageous,* and *War Room.* Stephen
thored the *New York Times* best sellers *The Love Dare* and *The Resolution for Men.*
so serves on the board of the Fatherhood CoMission. Stephen and his wife, Jill,
six children.

Kendrick is a screenwriter, actor, and movie director whose film credits
de *Facing the Giants, Fireproof, Courageous,* and *War Room.* Alex is a featured
erence speaker and coauthored the *New York Times* best sellers *The Love Dare*
he Resolution for Men. Alex and his wife, Christina, also have six children.

Parker has written more than fifty books for children, teens, and adults,
ding the bestselling Night Night series and two Christian Retailing's Best
d winners. Amy and her husband have two children.

Copyright © 2019 Kendrick Brothers, LLC
Published by B&H Publishing Group, Nashville, Tennessee
BHPublishingGroup.com
Illustrations © 2019 by B&H Publishing Group
978-1-5359-4985-9
Dewey Decimal Classification: 248.83
Subject Heading: SELF-REALIZATION / INDIVIDUALITY / CHRISTIAN LIFE

Printed in the United States of America.
1 2 3 4 5 6 · 23 22 21 20 19

Hello, friend!

If someone asked you to describe yourself, what would you say? Would you answer with your name, age, where you live? Maybe you thought of your favorite sport or an instrument you play.

What about who Jesus made you to be? Your identity in Christ. Did that come to mind? We hope so. But the truth is this world doesn't really care about that. Over and over we're told what we should look like, who we should be, and how we should spend our time and money. Our identity—who we are—has become what we are on the outside, right here and right now, instead of who we are on the inside, for eternity.

Well, we're here to turn the focus of identity right back where it belongs: on your heart and soul and mind, reflecting the glory of the very One who made you. You are His, you know. And when you look in the mirror and see *that*, when you see yourself for who—and *Whose*—you truly are, your entire mind-set, and your life, will change for an eternity.

We pray that as you read this book, you will begin to see yourself not through the lens of the world but through the eyes of Christ. Then and only then will you know your true worth, your true purpose, your true identity.

In Him,

Stephen and Alex

CONTENTS

WHAT IS IDENTITY?

"But you," He asked them, "who do you say that I am?"
—Matthew 16:15

Who are you? Nothing like a big question to get us started.

What is your identity? What does that even mean? How do you identify *identity*? Simply put, you could say, it's *who you are.* Right?

Sooo, who am I? Who are you? What makes you and me . . . *you* and *me*? What sets our identity?

These are pretty normal questions. In fact, Jesus asked His disciples similar questions. He asked what people were saying about Him, who people thought He was.

And the disciples said they had heard different answers. "Some say John the Baptist; others, Elijah; still others, Jeremiah or one of the prophets" (Matthew 16:14).

In this one simple passage, we learn several things from Jesus about identity. First, a lot of people had it all wrong. Obviously Jesus wasn't John the Baptist, or Elijah, or Jeremiah. He was Jesus.

Second, why do you think Jesus asked this question? Do you think Jesus was trying to figure out who He was? No. He was asking who *the people said* He was. Their answers—their wrong answers—said more about the people than they did about Jesus. Some people were more willing to believe Jesus was actually Elijah, a long-dead prophet, instead of believing Jesus was actually the promised Messiah, sent to save the world.

But just because they *thought* Jesus was John the Baptist certainly didn't make him John the Baptist. Just because they *said* he was Elijah absolutely did not make him so. And just because they *whispered* that he was Jeremiah did not turn Jesus into Jeremiah.

No, no, and no. Jesus is and was and will forever be *Jesus*. No matter what people think. No matter what people say. No matter how many people think it and say it.

Third, last, and maybe most important: *Jesus knew who He was.* He knew the truth. He knew who He was, who had sent Him, and what His purpose was here on planet Earth. And nothing, no thing, no person was going to change that.

WHY IS IT IMPORTANT?

Simon Peter answered, "You are the Messiah,
the Son of the living God!"—Matthew 16:16

If someone told me that I was an excellent basketball player, I can't say that I'd believe them. If someone tried to convince me that I was a long-lost prince, well, I'd probably just laugh at them. If someone told me that I should be a supermodel, I'd *know* they were joking. And I certainly wouldn't spend my life pursuing that modeling career.

Why? Because I know the truth. I know my identity. And while God created me to be lots of wonderful things, I am none of *those* things.

Your identity sets your course in this world, whether you know it or not. And if you don't know your identity, if you spend your entire life searching for it, trying everything the world tells you to do to "find yourself," you're going to follow a really zig-zaggy course that possibly leads to nowhere.

So let's get back to Jesus. The disciples had already told Him what "the people" were saying about His identity. Then Jesus turned to them and asked, "Who do you say that I am?" (Matthew 16:15).

Immediately Simon Peter replied, "You are the Messiah, the Son of the living God!" (v. 16).

Did those words turn Jesus into the Messiah? No. Did Jesus suddenly have His Messiah clothes and carriage, as if Simon Peter were a magical fairy godmother? Um, no. But with those words, Peter stated the truth about Jesus's identity. He showed that he understood who Jesus really was. And Peter demonstrated that he was someone Jesus could trust with His identity.

Through it all, however, whether people said Jesus was Elijah or the Messiah, Jesus knew who He was. He knew His identity. And that identity didn't change.

You see, not everyone in this world is going to tell you the truth about who you are. They're going to tell you who *they* think you are or who *they* want you to be. But that has everything to do with the world and very little to do with who you *really, truly* are.

This is why it is *so very important* that you know your identity, that you know who you are, that you know Whose you are, and that you know you were created for a purpose, to do good and godly works. This is the truth about your identity. And by knowing that truth, you'll be able to hear the words of the world and filter out the truth from the lies.

WHO SAYS WHO YOU ARE?

And Jesus responded, "Simon son of Jonah, you are blessed because flesh and blood did not reveal this to you, but My Father in heaven."—Matthew 16:17

You're awesome!"

"You're a loser!"

"You're wonderfully made."

Whew. That's a lot of noise. Out of all the voices telling us who we are, which one do we listen to?

We've already determined that the voices of the outside world aren't super reliable. But what about your friends? Shouldn't your friends know who you are? Or your family? They live with you. They've smelled your stinky feet and heard you singing in the shower. Surely *they* have a true picture of who you are. Right?

Well, the answer is really simple: you are who God says you are. No *ifs*, *ands*, or *buts*. No exceptions. If anyone says anything that disagrees with who God says you are, they are wrong. Period.

Okay, sure, maybe that answer is simple, but seeing it play out in everyday life is not *easy*. I mean, if you walked into school one day and everyone screamed "Loser!" that wouldn't be easy to forget.

And that is why this message is so important. That is why you *have* to know who you are. The world out there isn't always easy, and it isn't always kind. You're going to need an armor of truth to make it through. You're going to need wisdom and facts to make tough choices. You're going to have to be prepared, to learn to stand tall and sure in your identity.

Let's get back to Peter and Jesus. When Peter declared the truth about Jesus's identity, Jesus immediately knew the Source of Peter's wisdom. Jesus said to Peter, "Flesh and blood did not reveal this to you, but My Father in heaven" (Matthew 16:17). We trust that if God revealed the holy identity of Jesus to Peter, He'll reveal a little of our identities to us.

So that's what we're going to do. We're going straight to the Source. We're going to dig in to the truth of God's Word. We're going to see, with our very own eyes, what our Creator says about who we are. Because only in knowing who you are, Whose you are, and your purpose in this world will you become fully who God created you to be.

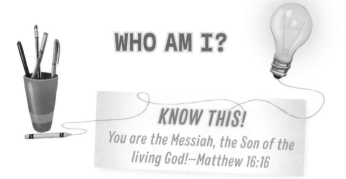

WHO AM I?

Before we dig in to what God says about you, take a few minutes to tell us what you already know about yourself.

Name: _____

Age: _____ Grade: _____

Height: _____ Weight: _____

Favorite color: _____

Favorite school subject: _____

Favorite movie: _____

Favorite thing to play: _____

The best things about me: _____

_____

I think that I am: _____

_____

God thinks that I am: _____

_____

Draw a picture of who you are.

THE WONDERS OF YOU

Did you know that more than 60 percent of human genes are identical to that of a . . . BANANA?![1]

1. https://www.getscience.com/biology-explained/how-genetically-related-are-we-bananas

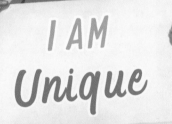

CHAPTER 1

CREATED BY GOD

You knit me together in my mother's womb. I will praise You because I have been remarkably and wonderfully made.
—Psalm 139:13–14

The first and very most important fact about your identity is this: you were created by God.

Yes, you!

It's hard to imagine, isn't it? The same God who dreamed up the seemingly infinite universe—with black holes and red giants and white dwarfs—made you. And you, dear one, have been so very wonderfully made.

You.

The same God who planned the world's river systems planned the path of your blood vessels. The same God who made the oceans of the world handcrafted your happy tears. The same God who created time and space made your heart beat a rhythm.

The same God who gave energy to lightning bolts also made the electrical impulses in your brain. The same God who looked at creation and said, "It is good," says the very same thing about you.

You know what all of this means, right? You're not just a simple human, not just another boy or girl. You are a miraculous, fascinating creation, handcrafted by God Himself. Your heart beats, your lungs breathe, and your brain learns *because He made them*.

He made *you*. We'll get into *why* He made you a little later, but first you have to know, you have *to believe*, that God. Made. You.

This is the foundation of your identity. This is the very beginning of your value. This is the very beginning of your purpose. You see, if you can believe that God made you, you know that you are wonderfully made. If you can believe that God made you, you know that you are priceless. And if you can believe that the Creator of the universe made you, you know that you are here to fulfill a purpose God planned for you long, long ago.

You are here, you are priceless, and you have a purpose because God made you.

Do you believe it?

WHO IS GOD?

The God who made the world and everything in it—He is Lord of heaven and earth and does not live in shrines made by hands. Neither is He served by human hands, as though He needed anything, since He Himself gives everyone life and breath and all things.—Acts 17:24-25

Paul spoke this definition of God to the people of Athens. The people of Athens were pretty mixed up about what they believed and what and who they should worship. Acts 17 says, "The city was full of idols" (v. 16). These people wanted to learn all the newest, coolest religious beliefs and practices. They didn't want to leave any of them out. They even had an altar "TO AN UNKNOWN GOD" (v. 23), just to make sure they had all the gods covered. When Paul saw that altar, he spoke boldly and told the people of Athens about the one true God they did not know.

Does that sound kind of familiar? If you listen to the ramblings of the world, you may hear a similar message. You may hear people preaching that Jesus is not the only way to heaven. Or you may hear scientists saying that God is not real. There are groups who will tell us that believing our God is the only god is wrong and hateful to other people.

Growing up in the middle of all these different messages can be confusing. It can be difficult to know who God really is and what we should believe. That's why we should dig back into the timeless truth of His Word.

The Bible says that God
- is the Creator of the universe (Genesis 1:1),
- is everywhere (Jeremiah 23:24),
- knows everything (Hebrews 4:13),
- is perfect and holy (Leviticus 19:2; Matthew 5:48),

- is love (1 John 4:8),
- knows you (Jeremiah 1:5; Luke 12:7), and
- has good plans for you (Jeremiah 29:11).

The Bible says a lot of other things about God too, of course. But this list is a great place to start.

And please understand: simply knowing *what* the Bible says is only the beginning. In Jeremiah 29:13, we hear the Lord declare, "You will seek Me and find Me when you search for Me with all your heart." Only when we seek God, look for Him, and search for Him in our lives can we truly see Him and know Him and understand who He is . . . and who *we are* in Him.

WHO ARE YOU?

From one man He has made every nationality to live over the whole earth and has determined their appointed times and the boundaries of where they live. . . . For in Him we live and move and exist, as even some of your own poets have said, "For we are also His offspring."—Acts 17:26, 28

Oddly, this question—"Who are you?"—can sometimes seem even more difficult to answer than "Who is God?" Am I right?

I am a [red/yellow/black/white/purple/green] [boy/girl] who loves to [play baseball/knit/sing at the top of my lungs/read in a corner/play with kittens/draw spaceships].

I guess those things are part of who you are and what makes you unique. But even that information doesn't really tell us *who* you are, deep down at your core, does it? Not really.

When you know your identity in God, in Christ, you at least have a starting point. You at least know that you were created by Him, a God who creates wonderful, fascinating things. He specially selected your race, nationality, family, gender, and personality to make you uniquely you. And when you look to the Bible, God's personal letter *to you,* you can discover a lot of things God says about you—and who you are.

He says that you

- are made in His image (Genesis 1:26),
- were created for a purpose (Ephesians 2:10),
- have special gifts (1 Corinthians 12:7–11),
- have everything you need (2 Peter 1:3),
- are chosen by Him (1 Peter 2:9),
- are the body of Christ (1 Corinthians 12:27), and
- are so loved (John 3:16).

I'd say that all of those things make you pretty important!

Even if you've lost your best friend . . . even if you're horrible at sports . . . even if you feel like you're messing everything up right now . . . every single thing that the Bible says about you—*that God says about you!*—is absolutely, undeniably true.

So when you're pondering the question "Who am I?" the best answer is: YOU ARE HIS.

And when you know that, really know that, everything else seems a lot less important.

TOGETHER WITH GOD

"And I also say to you that you are Peter, and on this rock I will build My church, and the forces of Hades will not overpower it."
—Matthew 16:18

Let's travel back to that earlier scene between Jesus and Peter. Jesus asked who people said He was. And Peter declared that Jesus is the Messiah. That's where we left them. Do you know what Jesus said back to Peter after that? Read the verse above

So in that short passage about identity, three things happened.

First, Peter declared Jesus's identity. He was sure of who Jesus was—and wasn't afraid to say so. Jesus is the Messiah, a Savior sent not only to the world but also to Peter, to be his personal Savior.

Once Peter declared this fact, Jesus replied by confirming Peter's identity, by telling Peter who he was. It sounds simple, "You are Peter." But there's something profound in that statement. This isn't some random guy speaking. This is Jesus, the Son of God. And I hear Jesus saying, "Yes, I am the Messiah. And now that you know who I am, I will show you who you are. You will know your true identity through Me."

Last, we see that Jesus was going to put Peter to work. "On this rock I will build My church" (Matthew 16:18). Did you know the word *petra* in Greek means "rock"? *Petra*, Peter. Jesus wasn't afraid of a little wordplay.

Jesus also meant business here. He told Peter, "The forces of Hades will not overpower it." If I were Peter, I might be having second thoughts about this whole "church" thing. It doesn't sound like it's going to be very fun. In fact, it sounds like there's going to be trouble. It sounds like Peter's identity, his work, his life is going to face some tough times.

And that is part of your identity too. Claiming your identity in Christ is wonderful and holy and right. It will also be challenging and trying and hard. Carrying out the work God has for you probably means the world won't always agree with you. But together with God, you can be sure that you will have everything you need.

THE TRUTH ABOUT ME

"Your word is truth."—John 17:17

When you get lost, when you start to wonder who you are, when you are confused by the many messages of this world . . . just remember those four words.

Your word is truth.

God's Word is truth. And it is so much more than letters printed on a page. Hebrews 4:12 says it like this: "For the word of God is living and effective and sharper than any double-edged sword. . . . It is able to judge the ideas and thoughts of the heart."

It is living. The Bible isn't a dusty, old book written by a bunch of now-dead men. It is the living Word of a living God. WOW. And to be honest, I can't explain just how. Who can? But God's words to us—recorded long, long ago—are just as important and apply just as perfectly to our lives today as they did to people living two thousand years ago!

Maybe that's because truth, real truth, God's truth, doesn't change. It isn't washed away by the latest fad. It isn't outshined by the newest gadget. It stands. It lasts. Because it is the truth.

It is also "sharp" and "effective." It works, and it works *well*. God's truth is sharp and strong enough to cut down any lie.

Finally, God's Word is *able to judge* the ideas and thoughts of your heart and the hearts of others. The more you know what's in the Bible, the better this works. But you can test every idea or thought against the truths of the Bible and see how it stands up. God's Word can judge whether those ideas are true and whether you should believe them, investigate them, or just ignore them.

The flip side of that, of course, is that *without* God's Word, without this perfect measuring stick of truth, you could believe just about anything you hear!

"You're worthless!" *Okay.*

"Elves created the universe." *Really?*

"If you draw purple pigs on your forehead, you'll live forever in the paradise of planet Pluton." *Dude, hand me that purple marker.*

But you know better. You've got His Word.

And His Word is truth.

I AM UNIQUE

LIES!

What are some things that have been said to you, or about you, that you *know* aren't true?

TRUTH!

Now look in your Bible (or back through this chapter). What is the truth about each of those things?

_____

_____

_____

_____

_____

_____

_____

_____

_____

_____

THE WONDERS OF YOU

You probably know that your fingerprints are unique. But did you know that your eyes, ears, lips, tongue, voice, toeprints, and teeth are all unique to *only you?*[2]

2. https://www.rd.com/health/wellness/unique-body-parts/

CHAPTER 2

I AM
Human

BORN A REBEL

For all have sinned and fall short of the glory of God.
—Romans 3:23

I don't know if you know this or not, but you come from a long line of rebels. And I don't mean that in a cool-mohawk kind of way. I mean that in a disobey-God kind of way.

Yeah. Not cool.

Alllll the way back to Adam and Eve, we've been messing up the perfection that God laid out before us.

"Don't eat from that tree."
"We ate from that tree." (See Genesis 3:13.)

"Follow Moses to freedom!"
"We wanna go back to Egypt!" (See Exodus 14:12; 16:3; Numbers 14:2; 21:5.)

"Trust Me to lead you."
"No, we want a king!" (See 1 Samuel 8:19.)

"Okay, here's My very own Son."
"Thirty pieces of silver? Sold!" (See Matthew 27:3.)

Not our finest moments.

But, like it or not, all of those things are part of our history as Christians. It seems so obvious, doesn't it? When we're looking back, reading about Adam and Eve, we're screaming, "Don't listen to the serpent! DON'T EAT THAT FRUIT!"

But it's not so obvious when it's you and me, here and now. We let the serpent slither around our necks, we listen to him telling us to try it, and sometimes, well, we do. You'd think that we'd learn. But we don't. We try to do better, but we still fall short.

Since that first bite of the forbidden fruit, we've proven ourselves to be pros at disobeying God. No matter what He does for us or how much He loves us, we still find a way to be ungrateful and disobedient. We're all rebels, all sinners, and we all fall waaay short of the glory of God.

And when we come to truly know this, who we are as sinners, we can begin to know who He is as God—an almighty, sacrificial Savior with a plan to bring His rebellious children home.

BUT GOD HAS A PLAN

But he was wounded for the wrong we did; he was crushed for the evil we did. The punishment, which made us well, was given to him, and we are healed because of his wounds.
—Isaiah 53:5 NCV

I magine you're standing in front of a window. The sun is shining so brightly that even with your eyes closed, you can still see the light. You feel its warmth on your skin, and the light fills the room.

Now imagine you pull a shade down over the window (you know, the plastic roller kind that rarely stays put and threatens to take off your nose as it snaps out of place. Wait, that hasn't happened to you?). You can still see some light coming through, but it's not as warm. Then you pull another shade over the same window. There's still some light, but no warmth. You pull another and another and another shade down until it's completely dark and a chill fills the room.

That's kind of what it's like when we sin in front of a purely holy God. God's holiness, His brilliance, is like the sun. It's not possible for us, as humans, to match it. And we could never absorb all His warmth. But we can be near Him, have His light shining down on our lives, and feel the warmth of His presence.

Then we sin. Sin separates us from God, like we're pulling a little shade down, separating us from His holiness, His warmth, His light. And we do it again and again—on purpose. We make choices that make us feel further and further away from the light of His love. After a while, with no way to lift the shades, we feel separated from God. And that is a very dark place to be.

God isn't surprised by our rebellion. He sees everything and knows everything. But He is holy. And we are not.

Still, for reasons we may never understand, God *wants* to be with us. He wants us unholy humans to stay in the presence of a holy God.

So He made a way: Jesus. Even before that precious Baby was born in a stable, God knew. God's only Son would carry the weight of our sins to a cross. He would die to pay the cost of our sins. A perfect Savior gave His life for our sins, and now He alone is able to lift all the dark shades of our sin, letting us once again stand fully in the light of our holy God.

Can you believe that? God loves us, wants us so much that He sent His only Son to suffer and die, just so He could be with us, so that we would be forgiven of our sins, so that we would live forever with Him in heaven. And we will—if only we believe in Him.

I MUST CHOOSE

Choose for yourselves today the one you will worship.
—Joshua 24:15

At some point you'll have to make a choice. It's a choice that will make a big impact on your identity. It's a choice that will make a big impact on your eternity.

Joshua and the Israelites had just witnessed the fall of the wall of Jericho. They had just entered the land that God had promised them. They had just reached the end of decades of wandering in the wilderness. And Joshua knew it was time.

"Choose for yourselves today the one you will worship," he called out to the Israelites (Joshua 24:15). He reminded them of their identity. He skipped back in time and told them the stories of where they had been, how far they had come, and how God had guided them, provided for them, every step of the way.

"Now, choose," he said. "Worshiping the one true God will not be easy. He will require your obedience. He will require your faithfulness. But He wants you to choose Him. And He will love you and provide for you, just as He has always done."

And if I may be so bold at this point in our journey, I'd like to ask you too. Whom do you choose to worship? Have you already decided? Are you still thinking about it?

Choosing God, following Jesus, is not easy. Joshua wasn't kidding! But if you've come this far, if you believe that He is your Creator, that you're a sinner, and that He has a plan to forgive you from your sins, well, is there really any other choice? Who else would we choose to follow, as children of God?

Still, God leaves it up to us. He's not going to force us to serve Him, to worship Him, to follow Him. But as our Creator, He knows this is the best way—it is the *only* way to truly live out our identities in the lives He created us to live.

AND I MUST NOT JUDGE

For when you judge another, you condemn yourself, since you,
the judge, do the same things.—Romans 2:1

Ouch. This is a tough one. I mean, how can you *not* judge the person who just called you an ugly word? Or the girl who's yelling at her mom in the church parking lot? Or the boy who is definitely lying about, well, you know . . . ?

Billy Graham, a man who dedicated his life to telling others about Jesus, explained it pretty simply: "It is the Holy Spirit's job to convict, God's job to judge, and my job to love." And take a look at Romans 2:1 above. When you judge someone else, you're condemning yourself. You're not only finding *that* person guilty, but you're only proving yourself guilty too.

When you think about it, what's the point of judging someone anyway? Why do we do it? Does it make you feel better about yourself? Does it make it easier not to like someone else? Does it

make it okay not to be friends with them? Does it cause you to sit back and think, *At least I'm not as bad as* that *person!*

Jesus told a little story about this very thing in Luke 18:9–14. He explained that two men went to the temple to pray. One was a Pharisee, a very well-educated teacher of the law of God. The other was a tax collector, usually known to be dishonest and greedy.

When the Pharisee prayed, he said, "God, thank You that I'm not a greedy sinner like that tax collector over there. I do all kinds of good stuff. I pray instead of eating. I give money to the church. . . ."

But when the tax collector prayed, he stood all alone and wouldn't even look toward heaven. He beat his chest and prayed desperately, "God, I am a sinner! Please save me!"

Which one do you think God looked at with more kindness? The Pharisee or the tax collector? See for yourself in Luke 18:14. But I'm guessing you already know.

Romans 3:23 reminds us, "All have sinned and fall short of the glory of God." *All*. The Pharisee. And the tax collector. And you. And me.

None of us is worthy enough, good enough, wise enough to judge another child of God. *Judge* is part of God's identity. But it is *not* part of ours.

SAVED OR LOST

*He Himself bore our sins in His body on the tree, so that,
having died to sins, we might live for righteousness.*
—1 Peter 2:24

Okay, so now we've covered how:

1. we are all sinners,

2. God has a plan to save us,

3. we must choose Him, and

4. we must not judge others.

But . . . why? Why would God save a bunch of sinners? What happens if we choose Him? Does it really matter?

Well, this is all part of our growing identity. And *this* is where we get to let God *change* our identity. This is where Abram became Abraham and Saul became Paul. This is where the criminal on the cross came to be with Jesus in paradise.

Jesus changes everything.

As the verse says above, Jesus died for us so that "we might live for righteousness." Well, there's a word with lots of syllables. Quick definition: to be made righteous is to be in good standing before God. When we choose Jesus, when we accept His offering of salvation, it should be just as obvious as when Clark Kent walks into a phone booth and Superman walks out. We begin to think differently, want differently, learn differently, and love differently. We turn our lives over to Jesus and live for Him. Jesus says, "If you love Me, you will keep My commands" (John 14:15). Plain and simple.

Choosing Jesus is not just a ticket into heaven. Choosing Jesus is a way to see heaven here on earth, right here and right now.

We begin to see people through the eyes of God. We begin to serve people as Jesus would. We begin to love as our Father loves us, *because* He first loved us (1 John 4:19).

When you live for Jesus, it is not just a *part* of your identity. It *is* your identity. You choose Him with everything you say and think and do. And in doing so, you choose the Creator who chose you first. You finally, truly become the YOU He created you to be.

When we choose Jesus, our identity changes from lost to saved, from living for ourselves to living to serve others, from floating around aimlessly to safe in the arms of God. There is no gray area. There is no fence riding. There is no lukewarm.

And no one can make that decision for you. Only *you* can choose to follow Jesus with your life.

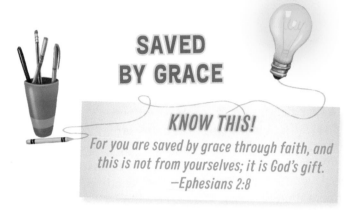

SAVED BY GRACE

KNOW THIS!

For you are saved by grace through faith, and this is not from yourselves; it is God's gift.
—Ephesians 2:8

In the space below, imagine yourself, your life, before choosing Christ. Either draw a picture or make a list of how you look, how you act, how you think, how you love.

Now imagine yourself after choosing Christ. Either draw a picture or make a list of how you would look, act, think, and love. How does Jesus change us?

THE WONDERS OF YOU

Did you know that a human produces enough saliva in a lifetime to fill two swimming pools?![3]

3. https://ohfact.com/interesting-facts-about-biology/

CHAPTER 3

A NEW LIFE

But God, who is rich in mercy, because of His great love that He had for us, made us alive with the Messiah even though we were dead in trespasses. —Ephesians 2:4–5

*E*ven though we were dead . . ."

Did you get that?

We were dead.

Before you choose a new life in Jesus—yep, it's true—*you're dead*. Simply put, "The wages of sin is death" (Romans 6:23). And without something to save us from our sins, we have no option but death.

Now, I know you don't *feel* dead or *look* dead, in a human sense. You talk and breathe and walk around. But in a spiritual sense, in a separated-from-God-by-your-sin sense, you are *very* dead.

Without Jesus, we are kind of like zombies, covered in the filth of our sin, arms outstretched, searching aimlessly for something to fill us, to feed us, to make us whole again.

Oh, but *with* Jesus . . . this real-life zombie movie has a happily-ever-after ending. With Jesus, we are given another chance—and not just any chance. With Jesus, we are given a chance at our absolute best life, a life with Him, fulfilling His purposes, for all eternity.

Once we choose Jesus, we are "made . . . alive with the Messiah" (Ephesians 2:5). Our eyes shine with a new purpose. Our hearts sing with a new joy. Our hands work toward His purposes.

It's a life so much more fulfilling than that icky zombie life we were living. It's the life we were always meant to live, a life with Christ in us. Then and only then is our life complete, the hole in our hearts filled with Christ. Only then are we really, truly alive.

A NEW SPIRIT

If anyone is in Christ, he is a new creation; old things have
passed away, and look, new things have come.
—2 Corinthians 5:17

Have you ever gotten a new laptop at your house?

If so, you probably noticed that it pretty much looks the same. It's rectangular with a screen and a keyboard, just like the old one. But you don't really get a new computer because of the outside—it's what's on the inside that is so different, so new.

It works differently. It's programmed differently. What comes out of it is different. It's faster. It's smarter. It's just better.

When you say yes to Jesus, the Bible tells us that we become "a new creation." But how? We look the same. We sound the same. We probably even smell the same. But that's just the outside.

Inside—in your spirit—you've been reprogrammed. Everything is different. You are a brand-new creation.

I know, I know ... you probably don't spend a lot of time thinking about your "spirit." But Jesus tells us, "God is spirit, and those who worship Him must worship in spirit and truth" (John 4:24). The spirit is a part of us that we can't see, but it's the part of us that connects us to God.

Before Jesus left His disciples on earth, He promised to send them the Holy Spirit as a helper. Just like our own spirits, we wouldn't be able to see the Holy Spirit. But we could feel it inside of us. That Helper would help us be aware of our sins and help us do what's right (John 16:7–8).

Now, that doesn't mean it'll be easy. That doesn't mean you'll automatically do everything right, the first time, just the way God wants you to. But it does mean that you'll have the guidance of the Spirit to walk alongside you, as a Helper for your own spirit as you connect with God.

When we choose Christ, we not only get the gift of eternal life—as if that weren't enough! We are also given a Helper for this life. We are all offered the gift of the Holy Spirit of God to guide us, to help us, to change us from the inside out.

A NEW DIRECTION

But if we walk in the light as He Himself is in the light, we have fellowship with one another, and the blood of Jesus His Son cleanses us from all sin.—1 John 1:7

Raise your hand if you like running around in total darkness. Not me. I am not a fan of bruises or stitches or late-night trips to the emergency room.

Now raise your hand if you like chasing fireflies. That's more like it! You wait stealthily for that little flash of light, then run toward it, waiting for the next clue. When it blinks again, you get a little closer, until finally it's lighting up your hands with its slow-blinking glow.

When you choose Jesus, along with a new life and a new spirit, you get a new direction. You go from running around aimlessly in the dark to chasing fireflies, to chasing the light.

First John 1:7 tells us pretty plainly that Jesus is right there, walking in the light. When we walk in the light, we walk with Him. Others are there too, walking with Him, walking in the light. And together, we are all free from sin.

But you can't say you're choosing Jesus and still run around aimlessly in the dark. You can't choose Jesus and still choose to do what's wrong, hiding from Him in the darkness. Well, I guess you can. But that's not really choosing Jesus. First John 1:6 says it like this: "If we say, 'We have fellowship with Him,' yet we walk in darkness, we are lying and are not practicing the truth."

So as you're traveling along on this journey with Jesus, be sure to check your direction on a regular basis. Are you just running around in the dark? Or are you chasing Jesus, chasing the light?

A NEW PURPOSE

But the fruit of the Spirit is love, joy, peace, patience, kindness, goodness, faith, gentleness, self-control.
—Galatians 5:22–23

What happens when you join a soccer team? You probably need new shoes and a uniform, maybe even some new clothes to practice in. Your schedule is going to change too. You'll need to be at practice twice a week, plus games. You'll go over the moves and plays in your head, remember what Coach taught you, and try to keep from doing that one thing that always trips you up. You'll probably even have a soccer ball with you most of the time, in case you want to kick it around, just for fun.

When you make those changes, after a while good things happen. You'll get more exercise and be healthier. You'll make new friends. You'll learn to be a better team member. And you'll probably even celebrate a few wins along the way.

Following Jesus is a lot like that. You'll make room for Him. You'll make changes in your schedule. You'll change the way you think, remembering what He said. You'll have Him there to guide you, to coach you through. And you'll probably want to keep His Word close by, so that you can learn more about Him whenever you get the chance.

And kind of like soccer, there will also be good things that come from a life of following Jesus. One list that the Bible gives us is called "fruit of the Spirit." When we spend our lives following Jesus, listening to the guidance of the Holy Spirit, we'll grow to have "love, joy, peace, patience, kindness, goodness, faith, gentleness, self-control" (Galatians 5:22–23). I don't know about you, but I could always use more of *all* those things!

Following Jesus is a practice. It's a way of life. It's something that, like any other practice, you show up and do every day.

And every day it makes you better. For eternity. When you choose Jesus, when you seek Him and follow Him every day, all of those good things—slowly but oh so surely—become a part of your identity in Him.

A NEW EXAMPLE

I no longer live, but Christ lives in me.
—Galatians 2:20

What do you want to do when you grow up? Do you want to be an astronaut? A firefighter? A teacher? A scientist? What do you dream of being? What is your goal? You can work toward any of those things, all of those things—or something entirely different.

When you're a Christ follower, there's another ultimate goal that you're always working toward: to be like Christ. The life of Jesus becomes permanently fused with your identity. Daily you are becoming a living, breathing, walking example of Christ for the whole world to see.

To maintain that identity, 1 John 2:6 tells us, "The one who says he remains in Him should walk just as He walked." To walk "just as" Jesus walked, well, that's a pretty tall order for anyone. Jesus was perfect in every way. And that makes Him a perfect example for us.

Hebrews 4:15 tells us that Jesus was "tested in every way," just like we are, and still, He did not sin. First Corinthians 10:13 also reminds us, "God is faithful, and He will not allow you to be tempted beyond what you are able, but with the temptation He will also provide a way of escape so that you are able to bear it."

All this talk about temptation and escape and being able to "bear it" sure makes this whole being-like-Christ thing sound like a lot of work, doesn't it? Well, it is. In the end, you know, Jesus gave His entire life for His Father's kingdom. And if we are really, truly Christlike, we will too.

But in doing so, we will also experience the beauty of His kingdom here on earth *and* in eternity. In our own way, we'll see His power at work in our lives. We'll see Him change the hearts of those we love. And we'll witness Him carrying us and loving us through it all.

To be clear, it *is* hard work. But so is being an astronaut. And I'd dare to say that the benefits of following Christ are even more beautiful and glorious than a life of floating through space. But, hey, you could always do *both!*

THE FRUITS

What kinds of fruit are produced by a life without the Spirit, without Christ? (See Galatians 5:19–21.)

_____

_____

_____

_____

_____

What kinds of fruit come from a life with the Spirit, in Christ?

_____

_____

_____

_____

_____

_____

THE WONDERS OF YOU

Did you know that your skin replaces itself every twenty-seven days?[4]

4. https://www.webmd.com/beauty/cosmetic-procedures-overview-skin#1

CHAPTER 4

LOVED BY GOD

*"As the Father has loved Me, I have also loved you.
Remain in My love."—John 15:9*

God loves you."

How many times have you heard those words? Seen them on a sticker with a big, yellow smiley face? Or on a button with little red hearts?

It's a phrase that you hear so much, you may never really think about it. Until now.

God. You know the One whose words created a three-million-mile-around ball of flaming gas? The One who choreographed the dance of the planets? The One who helps a starfish regrow its arms? The One who made volcanoes, oceans, and Mount Everest?

Bananas, dragon fruit, and watermelons? Hearts, brains, and eyeballs? Rainbows, blizzards, and fog? Yeah, that One. That's God.

Loves. Puppy kisses. Kitten snuggles. A baby's smile. A mama's hug. To adore. To cherish. To treasure. To never, ever, ever, ever want to hurt. To always want to be near. To give to. To sacrifice for. To give an only Son so that another may live.

You. Yourself. God's creation. Wonderfully made. Chosen. Treasured. Loved.

Put that all together, and it's only the very beginning of what those three words mean.

God loves you. *He loves you.* He really, truly loves you. *YOU.*

It's not a cheap phrase meant for only stickers and buttons. It's a truth as old as the universe. It was true before you were born. It'll be true a thousand years from now.

God loves you.

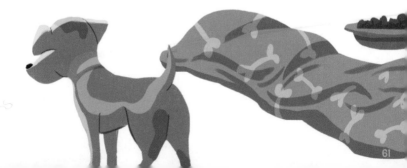

KNOWN BY GOD

Lord, You have searched me and known me.
—Psalm 139:1

In this psalm, David was realizing just how much God knew about him. He went on to say, "You know when I sit down and when I stand up. . . . You are aware of all my ways" (Psalm 139:2–3).

This was David the shepherd boy, David who defeated Goliath, and King David who made some pretty big mistakes. But God knew it all and loved him still.

You don't have to be King David for God to know you, though. He created us all and knows us all as His own. Jesus said that even as worthless as a sparrow seemed (five were sold for only two pennies!), God didn't forget a single one of them (Luke 12:6). He went on to tell the people, "Indeed, the hairs of your head are all counted," and "You are worth more than many sparrows!" (v. 7).

God doesn't only know the very hairs on your head. David said, "Before a word is on my tongue, You know all about it, Lord" (Psalm 139:4). He knows our very thoughts—before they even happen! Can you imagine?

Even before we were created, we were *known by Him*. "Your eyes saw me when I was formless; all my days were written in Your book and planned before a single one of them began" (Psalm 139:16). Did you realize that? Have you thought about *that*? God has been loving you before you were even you. He had plans for you before your parents did. You have always, always been known by and loved by God. *Even before you existed.*

It's hard for us to understand how much God really knows. In fact, it's impossible. We'll never fully understand.

But once David had wrapped his head around how much *he knew* that God knew, well, he just asked God to know him even more: "Search me, God, and know my heart" (Psalm 139:23).

David knew that God knew him best, better than he knew himself. So he asked God to show him things about himself that even he didn't know. And in doing so, David could continue to grow into the person God wanted him to be, the person God *created* him to be.

God knows us. We're not tricking Him with fancy prayers or our Sunday best. He sees all of us—the thoughts of our minds, the hairs on our heads, the plans yet to come. And He loves us.

And when we invite Him in to know more, to show us the truth of our hearts and lives, we can begin to grow into the person God created us to be.

CHOSEN BY GOD

For He chose us in Him, before the foundation of the world, to be holy and blameless in His sight.—Ephesians 1:4

Man, it feels good to be chosen. When all the kids raise their hands and the teacher points to you . . . when the smart kid wants to be your partner on the project . . . when your name is first on the list for the lead part in the school play . . . when it's time to pick teams and everyone turns to you . . .

Hmm, well, I *imagine* those things feel good. I wouldn't really know. I was rarely first on the list for *anything* when I was your age (or today). And that's okay.

You know why? School days, school friends, school competitions —they're temporary. In the blink of an eye, you'll be looking back at those days and laugh. (Grown-ups always say that, huh? But we always say that because *it's true*.)

And here's the even better news: whether you're chosen first or last, in school, at home, for the task, or for the team, it doesn't matter. Not really. It may look like it matters. It may *feel* like it matters. But when it feels that way, remember Ephesians 1:4.

No, seriously. Memorize it. Know it in your heart. It is part of your true identity.

Way before your school days, before school was invented— actually, before the world was invented—God chose you. He knew He would create us as humans—and He chose us. He knew we would sin—and He chose us. He knew He would have to give His very own absolutely perfect Son to save us—and He chose us.

Now, I don't know about you, but I'd say that's much more important than any team or school play or science project. So when you're feeling less than awesome, left out, or *unchosen*, remember, that's just not true.

Because *God* chose you.

ONE WITH GOD

You also are being built together for God's dwelling in the Spirit.
—Ephesians 2:22

Do you remember in the Old Testament when Moses was given instructions for building the tabernacle, the holy tent? God told Moses exactly how to build the place where God would "dwell" or come to be among His people. And Moses did exactly as God instructed him. (See Exodus 25–31; Numbers 7.)

The tabernacle was made up of the Holy Place and the Most Holy Place, separated by a "veil," a curtain made of the most beautiful fabric, embroidered with golden thread by creative artisans. The Holy Place contained a lamp, an altar, and a table, crafted by the most skilled craftsmen. The priests made sure the offerings were presented there according to the rules God gave them.

The Most Holy Place was where they put the ark of the covenant, the box holding the stones inscribed with the Ten Commandments. Even the highest priest could only enter there once a year. But this place, the Most Holy Place, the Holy of Holies, is where God dwelled among His people.

When God gave all these specific directions and rules—about how the tabernacle was crafted, about the offerings to be made— He wasn't trying to be difficult. He was making a point. He wanted His people to understand that the place where they would spend time with Him was sacred. It would be the most special, the Most Holy, worthy of a Most Holy God.

The Israelites understood and obeyed. They offered their best materials to build this holy place, so much that they had to be told to stop offering materials—they had given more than enough. Only the finest craftsmen were chosen to build and adorn the tabernacle with these materials. And God stayed there with His people.

Fast-forward to Jesus's time. On that dark day when He died on a cross, something happened: the temple curtain was torn in two. The Most Holy Place was no longer veiled. (See Matthew 27:51.) And God would come to live not only among us, but also within us, in our spirits. Through Jesus, we could finally be one with God; He would be living, or as Ephesians 2:22 says it, "dwelling," inside of us.

But with that "dwelling" also comes the question: How have you prepared His dwelling place? Have you crafted your spirit with the finest materials? Do you guard your heart, allowing only the Most Holy to enter? Do you continue to offer only your best to the One who is living there?

When we become one with God, we must remember that we become the home of the Most Holy, where only the finest and best will do.

BLESSED BY GOD

Praise the God and Father of our Lord Jesus Christ, who has blessed us in Christ with every spiritual blessing in the heavens.
—Ephesians 1:3

One of the ways that God shows us His love, that He shows us we are His, that He confirms our identity in Him, is through His many blessings. Ephesians 1:3 says He has blessed us with "every spiritual blessing in the heavens"!

But do you ever really sit and think about that? Do you ever look around at all your blessings and see just how incredibly loved you are?

We've talked about some of the biggies in this chapter. For one, you are absolutely loved by God. I honestly can't think of a bigger blessing than that. But you were also *created* by God, in His image. Think of the magnitude of that! You were *chosen* by God—the God of the universe *chose* you! And through Jesus, we are made *one with God*, the Holiest of holies.

As if those blessings weren't unbelievable enough, look around you. Look at your community, the park where you play, the grocery with endless kinds of food, the church where you worship.

Look outside your door, at the paved streets, the tall trees, the light of the sun (or the snow or clouds or the rain—they're all blessings!). Look at your home, where all your needs are met, where you're most comfortable, where memories are made. Look at your family, those who love you, help you, and encourage you. Look at your room, with photos of friends, posters of things you love, trophies you've earned, creations you've made. These are all gifts from the God who loves you.

What about the things you can't see? Those spiritual blessings? You are holding this book because someone cared enough about you to show you your true identity in Christ. Someone is praying for you daily. (I'm praying for you as I'm writing this.) Your pastor right now is preparing a sermon for you. Your heavenly Father is this very minute preparing a home for you in heaven. Your spiritual blessings, though unseen, can be the greatest blessings you'll ever know.

And all of these blessings—the seen, the unseen, the known, the unknown—are yours, because *you are His.*

GIFTS FROM GOD

KNOW THIS!

Praise the God and Father of our Lord Jesus Christ, who has blessed us in Christ with every spiritual blessing in the heavens.

—Ephesians 1:3

There is not enough paper in the world to list all the blessings God has given us, but we're going to start right here, right now. Write down as many as you can think of.

1. _____

2. _____

3. _____

4. _____

5. _____

6. _____

7. _____

8. _____

9. _____

10. _____

Now write a little note to God, thanking Him for all the many blessings He's given you—because He LOVES you.

_____

_____

_____

_____

_____

_____

_____

_____

_____

_____

_____

THE WONDERS OF YOU

Your heart beats 42,048,000 times in one year![5]

5. https://wonderopolis.org/wonder/
how-many-times-does-your-heart-beat-in-a-lifetime

CHAPTER 5

WITH HIS LOVE

*To all who did receive Him, He gave them the right
to be children of God. —John 1:12*

It's an undeniable part of your identity that you were created by God and that you live in a universe created by God. But so much more of your identity is that you are *loved* by God.

Still, God doesn't just love you like a friend or a nephew or a student. All of those are great. But none of them even comes close to being in the same realm of comparison as the way God loves you. Once you receive Christ, once you decide to follow Him, you become a child of God. And God loves you like you're His very own child—because you are.

Think about the way your mom looks at you as she sweeps your hair off your forehead. Think about the way your dad tries to give you everything you need. God loves you like this.

And. So. Much. More.

Jesus explained it to His disciples like this:

> What father among you, if his son asks for a fish, will give him a snake instead of a fish? Or if he asks for an egg, will give him a scorpion? If you then, who are evil, know how to give good gifts to your children, how much more will the heavenly Father give the Holy Spirit to those who ask Him? (Luke 11:11–13)

"How much more . . ."
As a child of God, you are given a vast inheritance. We'll talk about some of the things He gives you in this chapter: His grace, His power, His riches. And we'll also talk about the role you are called to play and the responsibility that comes with those gifts.

Your entire identity shifts when you realize that you are not only loved by God, but even more, a beloved *child* of God, an heir to the Creator of the universe. The whole world is His, and as His children, it is ours. It is a gift given generously and freely. But it is also a privilege that should not be taken lightly. I pray that we live our lives keenly aware of the honor of that incomparable title: child of God.

WITH HIS GRACE

We have redemption in Him through His blood, the forgiveness of our trespasses, according to the riches of His grace that He lavished on us with all wisdom and understanding.
—Ephesians 1:7–8

When we become a child of God, one of the first gifts He gives us is the richness of His grace. He takes all of our sins—no matter how big or small or seen or hidden—and He wipes them away, forgiving them completely, sending them "as far as the east is from the west" (Psalm 103:12).

Because of the death of a perfect, innocent Savior on a cross, God has an infinite storehouse of grace, just for us. All of the people in the entire history of the universe, sinning all of the sins there ever were to sin, multiplied by four billion and three, wouldn't even begin to use up God's storehouse of grace.

Now, before you get any big ideas: that doesn't mean we should take our sin lightly, that we should go around doing all the wrong things because we know there's an endless supply of God's grace. We should never forget that Jesus "was pierced because of our transgressions," wounded because of our wrongdoing (Isaiah 53:5). For all of the sins of all of the world, a great price was paid. But Jesus loves us so much that He gladly bore that piercing pain.

That's the extravagance of the gift of grace that God has given you. It's a gift we should forever be thankful for, a one-of-a-kind sacrifice we should never take for granted. It is an endless love we should spend our entire lives walking toward. And it is a gift that, when truly understood, fills us up and spills out onto everyone around us, covering everyone with the gift of His grace.

WITH HIS POWER

I pray that the perception of your mind may be enlightened so you may know . . . what is the immeasurable greatness of His power to us who believe.—Ephesians 1:18–19

The power of God is a gift that is sometimes misunderstood or overlooked completely—but not by you. Nope. Before we go anywhere, we're going to make sure you have a firm grasp on this gift of the power of God.

As a child of God, you have the ability to plug into His power. And when you begin to trust in God and His power, the magnitude only multiplies. You come to understand His plan and His purposes for your life, and working along with that plan and purpose, you harness the unimaginable force of God, working alongside you, clearing the obstacles, making the way for you to fulfill your God-given purpose. The obstacles of this world are defenseless against the awesome power of God.

- When we obey Him, He honors us (Exodus 19:5).

- When we face injustice, He stands beside us (Psalm 37:28).

- When we are weary, He holds us up (Isaiah 40:29).

- When we call on Him, He answers (Psalm 120:1).

But to even *begin* to fully understand the power that God offers to His children (sorry, but I don't think we'll ever *fully* understand it), you're going to have to get to know its Source. You have to spend time with God and in His Word. You have to get to know His character and what He expects from His children. When you align yourself with God and His purposes, the power inside of you is greater than anything in this world (1 John 4:4).

He wants you to come to Him with your needs. He wants you to let Him into your life. And when you do, He will blow you away with His loving power.

WITH HIS RICHES

Together with Christ Jesus He also raised us up and seated us in the heavens, so that in the coming ages He might display the immeasurable riches of His grace through His kindness to us in Christ Jesus.—Ephesians 2:6-7

What can you think of that's "immeasurable"? What is it that, no matter how you tried, you could never measure or count? The sand on the seashore . . . the molecules of oxygen in Earth's atmosphere . . . the amount of your love for jelly beans?

God's riches are immeasurable. I would dare to say those riches are even greater, wider, and more plentiful than the sand on the seashore. And He wants to share them all with us—the riches of His grace, the riches of His creation, the riches of His love. They are yours when you believe and trust in Him.

A word of caution here, though: God's idea of riches might be very different from our own. "God's riches" doesn't necessarily mean that a guy with balloons and a big, fake check is going to knock on your door. Although God completely understands the physical riches of this world—and sometimes rewards us in those ways—His greatest value is placed in things that are eternal. For instance, His grace, as in Ephesians 2:6-7. And the three things that last forever: faith, hope, love (1 Corinthians 13:13).

Jesus teaches us,

> "Don't collect for yourselves treasures on earth, where moth and rust destroy and where thieves break in and steal. But collect for yourselves treasures in heaven, where neither moth nor rust destroys, and where thieves don't break in and steal. For where your treasure is, there your heart will be also" (Matthew 6:19-21).

So as we step into our role as children of God, let's be sure to align our hearts and minds with the riches of God. Let's keep our eyes focused on the glimmers of grace, the wealth of faith, the sparkles of hope, the richness of love. Let's look to gather the immeasurable riches of those things that are eternal.

WITH A ROLE TO PLAY

*For we are His creation, created in Christ Jesus for good works,
which God prepared ahead of time so that we should walk in them.
—Ephesians 2:10*

If you could choose a starring role in any movie, what would
it be? Would you be a good guy or a bad guy? Would you wear
a ninja suit or a superhero cape? Would you carry a guitar or a
magic wand? Would your catchphrase be funny or strike fear in
your opponents?

I like to pretend as much as anyone, but here in real life, I
know that I already have a role to play. And it's way more important than any ninja or fairy godmother.

We are children of God. Of course, you already know that. But
have you thought about what that actually looks like? If you were
to make a film called *Child of God* (creative, I know), who would
be the star? How would the costume be designed? What would
the plot be? How would it end?

Well, Ephesians 6 gives us a great start:

Put on the full armor of God so that you can stand against the
tactics of the Devil. For our battle is not against flesh and blood, but
. . . against the spiritual forces of evil in the heavens. This is why you
must take up the full armor of God, so that you may be able to resist
in the evil day, and having prepared everything, to take your stand.
Stand, therefore,

with truth like a belt around your waist,
righteousness like armor on your chest,
and your feet sandaled with readiness
for the gospel of peace.
In every situation take the shield of faith,
and with it you will be able to extinguish
all the flaming arrows of the evil one.

Take the helmet of salvation,
and the sword of the Spirit,
which is God's word.
Pray at all times in the Spirit. (vv. 11–18)

In those verses we see the bad guy, the good guy, the costume, the plot, the conflict, and the resolution. Standing strong in God's armor, we will be prepared. We will be able to resist. And our faith will extinguish the flaming arrows of the evil one.

So much unhappiness in life comes when we play the wrong role, when we choose to act as someone other than a creation of God, created in Christ Jesus for good works. But knowing your role, wearing your costume, and listening carefully to your Director will give you the starring role in the life you were created to live.

CHILD OF GOD

KNOW THIS!
Put on the full armor of God so that you
can stand against the tactics of the Devil.
—Ephesians 6:11

So, how does a child of God look . . . think . . . act . . . live? On these pages, take a moment to design, draw, and label your costume or armor. Or maybe draw or describe a scene that might take place. Write some dialogue you might have, how you might react to a situation. Choose one way to show how being a child of God gives you a special identity in Him.

THE WONDERS OF YOU

Human bodies give off a tiny amount of light! You can't see it, but it's there. Shine bright![6]

6. https://natgeokids.com/uk/discover/science/general-science/
   15-facts-about-the-human-body/

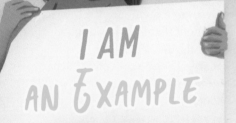

CHAPTER 6

I AM
AN EXAMPLE

IN MY ACTIONS

Do not let anyone treat you as if you are unimportant because you are young. Instead, be an example to the believers with your words, your actions, your love, your faith, and your pure life.—1 Timothy 4:12 NCV

Have you ever stood at a store counter, with money in your hand, only to be passed over for the adults behind you? I still remember what that feels like. When you're trying to learn to be independent and outspoken and resourceful, it's difficult when the whole world seems to look over the top of your head.

Jesus talked about this. When His disciples shooed a group of children away, Jesus told them, "Let the little children come to me, and do not hinder them, for the kingdom of heaven belongs to such as these" (Matthew 19:14 NIV).

Timothy apparently had issues in this department too. Paul wrote the verse above in a letter to Timothy, telling him that he needed to be a good example even though he was young. I have a feeling these words were written for you too.

Once you become a Christian, no matter how young or old, you become an example of Christ. You're not only representing your family or your school—you begin to represent God in everything you do. When people want to know what Christians look like, what they act like, how they treat others, they'll be looking at you.

I know it seems like a lot of pressure. God knows that too. That's why He gave us that big book of advice on how to live our best lives. But you don't have to memorize the whole book to be a good example. Jesus said quite simply, "If you love Me, you will keep My commands" (John 14:15). And when asked what the greatest commandment was, He answered, "Love the Lord your God with all your heart, with all your soul, and with all your mind. . . .

The second is like it: Love your neighbor as yourself" (Matthew 22:37, 39). That's enough to get you started anyway.

But this is also why God gave us grace. Jesus is the only perfect example we've got. So be prepared: you're gonna mess up. We all do. And when you do, you can use that as an example too. In fact, when you mess up, it's the best time to become a living, shining example of God's amazing grace. An imperfect person who is made perfect through Christ is the perfect example, the exact identity, of a Christian.

IN MY ATTITUDE

All bitterness, anger and wrath, shouting and slander must be removed from you, along with all malice. And be kind and compassionate to one another, forgiving one another, just as God also forgave you in Christ. —Ephesians 4:31-32

You've seen one of those remodeling shows on TV, right? They go in, get rid of all the ugly, worn-out stuff, and replace it all with clean, fresh, beautiful things. That's what happens on every single show. There's no plot twist, no switcheroo. People know what's going to happen, and still they watch. Why? We love to see the transformation. It gives us hope every time we see something old and ugly made new.

The verse above reminds me of one of those shows. But instead of a house, it's talking about me and you. It's talking about our attitude once Christ comes in and cleans us out.

Go into your mind right now and look around. Oh, there's some outdated bitterness in the corner over there. And in that room, what is that anger about? Jealousy? Dishonesty? Move 'em out. Take it all and throw it in that big dumpster out front. Those things don't belong here anymore.

Now let's go gather some kindness and compassion. Let's build up some laughter and generosity. Let's paint all the walls with forgiveness. And let's live in this beautiful new home that Christ has provided for us.

When you start to feel anger building up, deal with it. Sweep it out the front door. Remember the grace and compassion that God has shown to you, and let it overflow onto everyone around you.

Your attitude, the way you look at the people and the world around you, is an example of the God who saved you. A rotten, yucky heart is not a reflection of someone who has been cleansed by Christ. But a forgiving, compassionate heart is an example of the God who saved you—and points others to Him as well. So go star in your own remodeling show by showing others the transformation that Christ has made in you!

IN MY WORDS

But speaking the truth in love, let us grow in every way into Him who is the head—Christ.—Ephesians 4:15

"Trash in, trash out." Ever heard someone say that? I say it often to my kids as a guide for the things they listen to or watch.

Think about all the words you consume each day. The words streaming through your earbuds or the things you watch on YouTube. The posts you tap on social media. The voices in the hallways, lunchroom, and classrooms at school. The words you read in black and white on the page or that flash across the screen in video games or commercials. All these things are feeding your brain.

There are basically three things you can put in your brain: nourishment, junk, and poison. Of course, the nourishment—reading your Bible, math and English, kind words with a friend—all of those words (and numbers) are great for your brain. They help it grow.

Then there's the junk: the videos of other kids playing on YouTube, the mindless shows on TV, or leveling up in video games. You know when it's junk, just like you know a donut is junk. It's not nourishment, but it's okay in small amounts.

The poison, though, is the stuff you want to avoid at all costs.

You would never turn up a bottle of rat poison and say, "Hmm, just a little bit won't hurt." It's the same with the stuff that poisons your brain. Sometimes, though, we don't think of it that way. Sometimes we see other people doing it and think it's okay. But gossip, hatefulness, violence, lying, bad words, making fun of people, and all those other things you *know* you're not supposed to be watching or hearing—no matter how cleverly they're disguised—are all just poison for your brain.

Trash in, trash out. Whatever you feed your brain is going to determine what comes out of your brain. And there's already enough trash in this world.

As Philippians 4:8 tells us, "Finally brothers, whatever is true, whatever is honorable, whatever is just, whatever is pure, whatever is lovely, whatever is commendable—if there is any moral excellence and if there is any praise—dwell on these things." (Also see Ephesians 4:25, 29.) Let *these* be the things you use to feed your brain. And let *these* be the words you use to build your identity in Christ, both for yourself and for those who are looking to you as an example.

6: *I AM* AN EXAMPLE
IN MY RELATIONSHIPS

From Him the whole body, fitted and knit together by every supporting ligament, promotes the growth of the body for building up itself in love by the proper working of each individual part.—Ephesians 4:16

All the things we've talked about so far in this chapter—your actions, your attitude, your words—have a big impact on your relationships. And all the Scripture we've quoted so far could be applied to your relationships as well. There's a good reason for that.

God made us. God *knows* us. He knows our needs and what makes us happy. And when we follow Him and His design, well, *everything* is better—especially our relationships. Families, marriages, friendships, they all grow when built on a godly foundation, when we follow God's instructions for taking care of the people He made.

One of the Ten Commandments is about the most important human relationship in your life right now: "Honor your father and your mother so that you may have a long life in the land that the LORD your God is giving you" (Exodus 20:12). He didn't tell you this because all parents are perfect and deserving of honor. He commands this because He knows that this is the best way for this relationship to grow. He knows that this is best for both your parents and you.

After all, your "long life" depends on it! As crazy as it may seem sometimes, God chose those people to be your parents. And believe it or not, those parents are wiser than you. When He made you, He knew exactly what you would need to grow into the person you would need to be. He crafted those people and gave them to you. And in His Top Ten Rules, He tells you to honor them. When you dishonor them, you dishonor God. And when you honor them, you honor God, simple as that.

But honoring your parents and your relationships is about more than just a "do and don't" list. Take a look at the verse above. Something important happens when we treat others the way we're supposed to. "The body" is talking about the church, and "every supporting ligament" and "each individual part" is talking about you and me. When we honor our relationships with our actions, our attitudes, and our words, when we "support" and "build up" the people around us, we are building God's church. We are making it stronger. We are helping it grow. And isn't that really what we're here for? Isn't that really the most important thing ever in this life?

Be an example in your relationships. And then just watch how—*together*—we can grow.

IN MY BELIEFS

*Then we will no longer be little children, tossed by the waves
and blown around by every wind of teaching.*
—Ephesians 4:14

I'm just going to tell you straight: this is a tough one. You would think after a couple thousand years of being on this planet it would get easier to be a Christian, to be an example in your beliefs. But it hasn't. And it doesn't.

Of course, God knew this. Prophets spoke of this. Jesus told us about this. In Matthew 24:9, He said, "You will be hated by all nations because of My name." (Read the entire passage in Matthew 24:3–14.)

But I can't help but wonder: How can we make it better? Is it difficult partly because we aren't doing what the very title of this section suggests? Are we all doing our best to be an example in our beliefs? And if not, why not?

Maybe we need to go back to the basics. Maybe we need to go back and rediscover what our beliefs *are*. Only when we *know* what our beliefs are can we truly stand confidently in those beliefs. Or as 1 Timothy 4:7 says, "Have nothing to do with irreverent and silly myths. Rather, train yourself in godliness." Train yourself in His Word.

How will we ever know the truth from the myths of this world if we are not trained in it? And then, knowing that truth, we can stand confidently with answers about our faith. We can be a strong example in our beliefs.

Now, don't get me wrong here. Standing strong in your beliefs does not mean beating people over the head with your Bible. Once at a football game, there was a guy screaming important biblical truths—*nonstop*—through his megaphone. Although I appreciated the words he was saying, he was just annoying everybody. No one was listening. Everyone was avoiding him. And I'm not really sure that's the way Jesus would have done it.

Jesus loved people. He listened to their needs. He showed them how much He cared about them. And then they were really interested in the things He had to say about the kingdom of God. They knew that Jesus loved them and wanted what was best for them.

As Ephesians 4:21 so simply states, "The truth is in Jesus." And when we seek and find that truth in Him, our beliefs stand the strongest. Our lights shine the brightest. Our love shouts the loudest. And we are a strong example of our beliefs.

THE *BEST* EXAMPLE!

KNOW THIS!

Do not conform to the pattern of this world, but be transformed by the renewing of your mind. —Romans 12:2 NIV

Being an example for Christ is a continual work in progress. You're constantly moving out the old and replacing it with the new truths that you're discovering in Him. So let's have some fun with it.

On this page, draw your old house, filled with old habits, old thoughts, and old beliefs. Label each of them as you show us your yucky, old house.

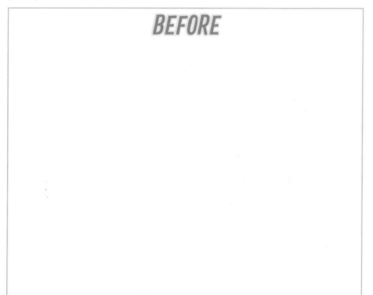

BEFORE

Now reveal the new house—the transformed you, what you're doing and thinking and believing to build the best example you can be!

AFTER

THE WONDERS OF YOU

Did you know that your body is constantly renewing itself? You get a new skeleton every ten years![7]

7. https://www.businessinsider.com/
how-long-it-takes-the-body-to-grow-hair-nails-cells-2018

CHAPTER 7

EVEN WHEN I FEEL LIKE IT

"Do not be afraid or discouraged, for the LORD your God is with you wherever you go."—Joshua 1:9

Think about a time when you felt alone. I mean *really* alone. Maybe there were tears. Maybe there were bad thoughts. Whatever it was, you felt like no one understood and no one could help.

Our feelings can be really powerful. They can make us do stupid things. They can make us do really wonderful things. But we have to know the difference. And we have to know that in the end, feelings are just that: *feelings*.

Feelings aren't a bad thing, of course. God gave us feelings and emotions as tools to help us survive, to relate to others. They tell us when a friend needs a hug or a pat on the back. They let us mourn loss and celebrate victory. These are all very real, very healthy, very normal things.

But just like any other tool, feelings can be misunderstood and misused. If you use a screwdriver to eat your cereal, you won't get very far. If you celebrate things that are wrong, if you ignore someone's hurt, if you pull up a chair and sit in the muck of anger, your feelings can get you into trouble. And they can lead you to believe things that aren't true.

Now think back again to that time when you *felt* really alone. Where were you? At school? At home? What was around you? Who was there? I'm guessing that when you *felt* really alone, when you *felt* completely misunderstood, that was a feeling that wasn't very true. I'm guessing that maybe you were at school and there were three other kids feeling exactly what you were feeling. Or maybe you were home, and your dad was downstairs, wondering how he could help you. Or maybe—not *maybe*, I know this without a doubt—God was right there, watching over you, waiting for you to bring the problem to Him.

The truth is: no matter what your feelings tell you, you are *never, ever* alone. EV. ER. Jesus told His disciples, "And remember, I am with you always, to the end of the age" (Matthew 28:20). "Always." The interesting thing is: He said this just before *leaving* them, just before His physical body went back to heaven, leaving His disciples on earth. He said this because He knew. Jesus *knew* that His disciples would feel abandoned, misunderstood, deserted. That they would feel alone.

But Jesus also knew that they would never really be alone— even when they felt like it.

EVEN WHEN I'M TOLD THAT I AM

"When he tells a lie, he speaks from his own nature, because he is a liar and the father of liars."—John 8:44

Satan. The serpent. The devil. He is a sneaky, crafty soul. And he delights in nothing more than making God's people feel alone . . . afraid . . . unloved. He knows that people who feel alone, afraid, and unloved become desperate. And desperate people will do desperate things. They become putty in the hands of an evil creature.

Think about the first time we met this creature, way back in the garden of Eden. We don't see him making an announcement about this fruit to both people in the garden. No, we see him speaking only to Eve. And what did he tell her? That God had lied to her, that God didn't want Eve to be as smart as He was. After that, Eve looked at the fruit again. And this time she saw that it was "delightful" and "desirable" (Genesis 3:6). So she took a bite.

Satan had simply spoken those feelings into being. By whispering into Eve's ear, he changed her perspective. And because she listened to him, she looked away from God and toward her own selfish desires. This didn't take years or months. It happened in an instant. Just like that, she was bending to the whims of the devil.

That's not who you are. That is *not* your identity. Yes, absolutely, we are descendants of Adam and Eve. But we are *children* of God.

Satan is no dummy. He knows that he is absolutely defenseless against the power of God. But he also knows that if he can pull God's people from His power, if he can whisper into our ears and have us look away just for a moment, well then, anything is possible.

Guard your heart, dear one. Guard your heart. "For our battle is not against flesh and blood, but against the rulers, against the authorities, against the world powers of this darkness, against the spiritual forces of evil in the heavens" (Ephesians 6:12). And we cannot let down our guard. Not even for a second.

When you hear the tempting whispers of a charming voice calling your name, telling you that there's something bigger and better and more welcoming than the arms of God, turn away. Turn away and be held by the One Who knows you, Who loves you, and Who has already defeated the darkness of this world.

EVEN WHEN IT LOOKS LIKE IT

But know this: Difficult times will come in the last days.
—2 Timothy 3:1

The "last days"—it sounds like something out of a sci-fi movie, something that would require a lot of special effects, not something we would read about in the Bible. But it's all right there in 2 Timothy.

None of us knows when the "last days" will be. But this scene from chapter 3 sure does sound like the present-day world. The passage above goes on to say:

> For people will be lovers of self, lovers of money, boastful, proud, blasphemers, disobedient to parents, ungrateful, unholy, unloving, irreconcilable, slanderers, without self-control, brutal, without love for what is good, traitors, reckless, conceited, lovers of pleasure rather than lovers of God, holding to the form of godliness but denying its power. Avoid these people!
> (2 Timothy 3:2–5)

That's a pretty accurate description of the nightly news, isn't it?

But do you know the *good* thing about all of those horrible things? Those words are right there in God's Word. In fact, they were written a long, long time ago. And that tells me that whatever is coming, whenever it's coming, God is ready. He knew about all of these things long before they ever came to be. And His people—you and me—can be ready too.

When you hear scary things on the news . . . when your faith is frowned upon . . . when it seems as if everyone is doing the wrong thing and getting away with it—or even getting praise for it . . . turn your eyes to God, the One who knows and has always known. He is right there, waiting for you. And you are never, ever alone— even when it looks like it.

EVEN WHEN I MESS UP

The Lord disciplines the one He loves.
—Hebrews 12:6

Have you ever watched a cartoon character make an important decision? Suddenly a tiny angel and a tiny devil are sitting on each shoulder, telling all about the good and bad of the decision that's about to be made. Each one tries to persuade him, until finally the character makes the decision, and either the angel or the devil celebrates.

Of course, this is just a silly cartoon, but it's not too terribly far from the temptations we face in real life. When the serpent was tempting Eve in the garden of Eden, God was there too, even if Eve didn't see Him. (See Genesis 3.) If she had just turned her head toward Him, asked God for His help, for His input, there may have been a very different ending to that story.

First Corinthians 10:13 promises, "God is faithful, and He will not allow you to be tempted beyond what you are able, but with the temptation He will also provide a way of escape so that you are able to bear it." If you'll listen—*really listen*—you will hear Him. There will be a tug in your heart or a whisper in your mind telling you which way to go, the right way to turn, if you will only listen. Even there, in the midst of your temptation, when you're actually making that decision between right and wrong, God is there with you.

And afterward, whatever decision you make, He is there too. Of course He would prefer it if we made the decision to walk toward Him. The godly choice is better for us and everyone around us.

But even when we don't, even when we mess up, even when we choose to take a bite of the only fruit that He told us not to touch, He is still there. He still loves us. He is still willing to scoop us up into His arms and whisper, "Try again." And that's exactly what we need to do.

Even when you mess up, even when you don't feel like it, you are loved by the Creator of the universe, the Creator of *you*. You are so much more than "not alone." You are cherished and treasured and adored by the One who knows you the best, loves you the most, and wants the greatest things from you and the life that He has given to you.

Choose wisely. Make the most of it. And know that you are so much more than never alone.

HE IS WITH ME ALWAYS

"And remember, I am with you always, to the end of the age."
—Matthew 28:20

There are tons of valuable truths in the pages of your Bible. Jesus told so many important parables, performed so many astounding miracles. There are so many stories of faith and hope and courage.

All of those truths, all of those stories, come together to form one of the most important things Jesus asks you to remember: "I am with you always." You are never alone.

If you remember that, you don't get all wrapped up in your feelings. You'll turn to Him for help. If you remember that, you will go to Him instead of lashing out in anger. If you remember that, you will never feel desperately alone. Because you will know that He is with you.

God has sent those reminders to us all through the Bible, through the stories of His people. Please read them and know them. He sent a rainbow to Noah's family. He rained manna down on the Israelites. He sent ravens to feed Elijah. He sent Jesus to save us all.

As if that weren't enough, in the absence of His human body, Jesus sent the Holy Spirit as a helper for us. He will guide us to make the right decisions. He will give us strength and hope. He will help us to pray when we can't even find the words (Romans 8:26). He is not a physical human we have to look for because He is always there in our hearts. *Never alone.*

And if somehow, some way, we forget all that and wander out into this world with no knowledge of our Savior, there He is again . . . in the song of a chickadee, in the warmth of the wind, in the bloom of a buttercup . . . He is there. He is always. He is there.

This is our story, the story of God's people who are led and loved by an ever-present God. This is your identity, a child of God, who is never alone and never has to be separated from the power of an Almighty God. When you know these truths and hold them in your heart, really, what isn't possible for you? What is there that you cannot do, beloved child of God?

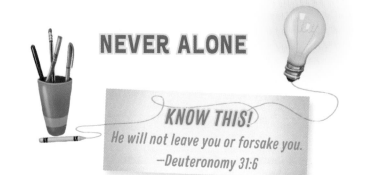

NEVER ALONE

KNOW THIS!
He will not leave you or forsake you.
—Deuteronomy 31:6

Story Title:

Noah, Joshua, Elijah, Moses and the Israelites, even Adam and Eve—we've talked about a few stories where God showed His people that He was always with them, no matter what. Which one is your favorite? Take a minute to find that story in the Bible and read it straight from there. On these two pages, illustrate your favorite scene or verse from the story. Then share that story with someone today. Let them know that they are never alone.

THE WONDERS OF YOU

Did you know that your brain is always working? Sometimes it's even more active when you're sleeping than when you're awake![8]

8. https://natgeokids.com/uk/discover/science/general-science/
15-facts-about-the-human-body/

CHAPTER 8

I AM
Called

TO LOVE HIM

"If you love Me, you will keep My commands."
—John 14:15

How do you know a football player is a football player? Is it the uniform? Well, that certainly *looks* like a football player. Maybe if all his friends are football players? Could be. Or maybe if his name is printed in the program at the football game? That makes him a football player, right?

Well, all those things are *likely* if you're a football player. But only one thing makes you a football player: playing football. And in the same way, Jesus said, "By this all people will know that you are My disciples, if you have love for one another" (John 13:35).

As Christians, we are called to love Jesus, to worship God. And that's not very hard to do, considering all that He's done for us.

But if we are truly His disciples, we have to love others too.

This is where it gets difficult. By love, Jesus didn't just mean "tolerate." Jesus gave the instructions to love others just *after* kneeling to wash His disciples' feet and just *before* being arrested and beaten and hung on a cross to save you and me. In the most obvious, sacrificial way possible, He showed us how to serve. He showed us how to give. And He showed us how to love.

Kneeling on the ground, head bowed, with dirty, stinky feet in His hands, He washed them clean. The King of kings washed the feet of ordinary men. Then He said simply, "You also should do just as I have done for you" (John 13:15).

No matter what our gifts or talents lead us to do, the center of our identity is this calling.

And Jesus will know us, the *world* will know us, by how we love each other.

TO WORSHIP HIM

*Our Lord and God, You are worthy to receive glory and honor
and power, because You have created all things.
—Revelation 4:11*

What do you think worship is? It's one of those words we use a lot but don't really think about its meaning, isn't it? Is worship when you sing at church? When you bow to pray? When you write a poem about the gifts God has given you?

Yes. Yes. And yes!

Worship is honoring God, respecting His presence and His power. It's about gratitude. It's about His greatness. It's about His never-ending love.

Worship is whatever you do to show God the gratitude and honor and respect He's worthy of. It's singing at the top of your lungs at church. It's sitting for a moment of silence alone. It's painting a beautiful picture. It's whispering "thank You" for a sunset. It's taking care of your body, your temple. It's keeping the Sabbath holy.

Worship is not something we save for Sundays. Worship is for the days when you consider God worthy of worship. And that is *every* day.

Worship is not for show. It is not for the benefit of others. Worship is for an audience of One. It is between you and God, for you to tell Him just how much you love Him.

Worship is not to make God feel good about Himself. Worship is not because God needs an ego boost. Worship is to remind us always of who created us, who we answer to, who is guiding us, who is watching over us, who *loves* us.

When we lift up the name of the Lord, we are lifted up too, because we remind ourselves of the greatness of the One who loves us so.

TO TELL OTHERS ABOUT HIM

I will make known the Lord's faithful love and the Lord's praiseworthy acts, because of all the Lord has done for us.
—Isaiah 63:7

The last instruction that Jesus gave to His disciples (right before reminding them "I am with you always") was "Go!"

Okay, more specifically, "Go, therefore, and make disciples of all nations, baptizing them in the name of the Father and of the Son and of the Holy Spirit, teaching them to observe everything I have commanded you" (Matthew 28:19–20). So, in other words, "Go, tell them about Me! Tell them how to *really* live life to the fullest!"

It's what Jesus asks you and me and *all* His disciples to do. He knows how important we are in this process. He saw how the crowds formed after the word spread about Him, about His power, about His miracles, about His grace. And He knows that the world today needs to hear about Him just as much as the people did two thousand years ago.

This is no small task. This is not a task you can blow off. This is not a task you can leave for someone else to do.

God has put you where you are, right there in the circle of people you're in, to make a difference. He knows that only you can get through to those particular people, at this particular time. He knows that only you will whisper His truths to them in the voice they need to hear.

This is up to you.

But don't tell others about Him because you *have* to. Don't do it because you'll get some awesome reward. Do it because you mean it, because you can't help but tell others about what He's done for you. When the joy that cannot be contained spills out onto the people around you, they can't help but want to know more about Him.

TO BRING GLORY TO HIM

We know that all things work together for the good of those who love God: those who are called according to His purpose.
—Romans 8:28

We are called, because of our identity as children of God, to bring glory to Him. This means, of course, that we will win all the trophies, we'll be the best looking people in class, life will always be perfect, and we will be rich and famous and popular. Right?

Eh . . . wrong.

First, the things that bring glory in this world are not necessarily the same things that bring glory to God. In fact, those things are usually quite the opposite, aren't they? Being honest and faithful, serving others, putting others before yourself, giving all that you've got to God—these things bring glory to Him. And these things aren't really going to make everything go smoothly for you all the time. Sometimes it will look like everyone doing the wrong things is getting all the glory and you're getting all the yuck.

Should I tell you? . . . It gets worse. Worse than not winning all the time, Christians are often persecuted—in the Bible *and* today. Jesus and His disciples had a lot to say about persecution (being treated badly because of their beliefs). All through the Bible, the prophets, the disciples, and even Jesus were all mistreated. And Jesus said, "If they persecuted Me, they will also persecute you" (John 15:20). Long after Jesus had left him, Peter said, "If anyone suffers as a 'Christian,' he should not be ashamed but should glorify God in having that name" (1 Peter 4:16). Even in persecution, even when we are mistreated *because* of Jesus, we are to glorify Him.

Are you ready for the good news? All of this, all of the bad, is, well, good. How? I don't know. But somehow, in ways that only God understands, He makes all of it—all the good, all the bad, all the persecution—work out for the good of those who love Him.

Through it all, we are to respond in a way that brings glory to Jesus, in a way that shows the world that we are His and He is good. When the bad comes, "the joy of the LORD is your strength" (Nehemiah 8:10 NIV). And when the good comes, "humble yourselves" (1 Peter 5:6). But in everything, in your actions and your emotions, bring glory to Him.

TO SERVE THE NEEDS OF OTHERS

God has shown you his grace in giving you different gifts. And you are like servants who are responsible for using God's gifts. So be good servants and use your gifts to serve each other.
—1 Peter 4:10 ICB

What gifts do you have? What do you really love to do? Bake brownies with Mom? Plant flowers in the yard? Fix stuff around the house with Dad? Draw pictures? Write stories? Play the trombone?

All these things can be a hint toward the gifts God has given you. First Corinthians 12 lists several different kinds of gifts: wisdom, healing, faith, languages, and more! And although these can look very different, they all come from the same Spirit and for the same purpose: to serve others!

Although our gifts can bring us lots of joy, they're not only meant for that purpose. They're meant to be shared with others too. The verse above tells us that we are "responsible for using God's gifts." And using these gifts to serve others makes us "good servants."

Being a good servant seems like the right response to the generosity of God's gifts, doesn't it?

When we use the gifts God has given us for His purposes, it all goes back to bring glory to Him. Matthew 5:16 says it like this: "In the same way, let your light shine before men, so that they may see your good works and give glory to your Father in heaven." While we're having fun using our gifts, making other people happy, it all brings glory to Him. I call that a win-win-win. Don't you?

Take some time to think about how you can use your gifts. You could take those brownies to a neighbor who's been sick. You and Dad could go fix Grandma's sink. Or you could put on a trombone concert for the seniors' home down the road. Jesus taught us that when we're serving others, we're actually serving Him (Matthew 25:40). And when you picture Jesus there, taking that plate of brownies with a smile, serving others takes on a whole new meaning.

Whatever you do, just be sure you don't keep those gifts all to yourself. Share them with others. Spread the joy. And more often than not, you'll find that you enjoy it just as much as the people you serve.

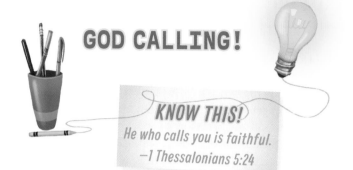

GOD CALLING!

KNOW THIS!
He who calls you is faithful.
—1 Thessalonians 5:24

If God were to call you on the phone, what do you think He would say? What do you think He would be calling you to do? Write out the conversation between you and God. And think of some ways that you can live out your God-calling every day!

THE WONDERS OF YOU

The electricity produced by your
brain could power a small light bulb![9]

9. https://www.rd.com/health/wellness/brain-facts/

WHO I AM !

WITH GOD WATCHING OVER ME

For I am persuaded that not even death or life, angels or rulers, things present or things to come, hostile powers, height or depth, or any other created thing will have the power to separate us from the love of God that is in Christ Jesus our Lord!
—Romans 8:38–39

We're reaching the end of this book, and I feel all this pressure to make sure you know . . . to take you by the shoulders and look you in the eyes and say, "Do you understand me?"

Do you know how much you are loved?

Do you know that you are never alone?

Do you know that you are unique and creative like your Creator?

Do you know that you are wonderfully made beyond belief?

Do you understand?!

This world is going to hit you. Hard. This world is going to tell you that everything you believe is not true. This world is going to tell you that you are stupid and ugly and worthless and just not enough. This world is going to tell you to give up and give in.

Don't listen. Okay? Don't you listen for a second.

The Creator of heaven and earth adores you. Your heart. Your soul. Your bones.

He is watching over you every second of every day, and there is nothing—NOTHING—that can separate you from Him. Do you understand me?

He is your God. And you are His.

That is *who you are*. That is your identity. And there is nothing in this world that can change that.

WITH THE WORD TO GUIDE ME

*All Scripture is inspired by God and is profitable for teaching, for
rebuking, for correcting, for training in righteousness, so that
the man of God may be complete, equipped for every good work.
—2 Timothy 3:16-17*

Even if you believe every single thing in this book, even if you
know it to be true, you're going to have questions. You're going
to sometimes feel like there are no easy answers. And sometimes,
well, there aren't.

But you have a vital resource right there, just waiting for
you to use it—the Bible! You have this timeless book of wisdom
you can pick up at any time, flip through its pages, and have the
wisdom of the omniscient God at your fingertips. Use it.

The verse above describes just how useful it is "for teaching,
for rebuking, for correcting, for training." We read it and know
it so that we may be "equipped for every good work." But most of
all, we understand it so that we "may be complete." It contains the
key to your heart, to God's heart. It's the secret to the life we long
for, to the identity we were meant to fulfill.

Of course, we'll never know that if we never pick it up, if we
leave it collecting dust on our bookshelves. And really, there's no
excuse for that.

Excuse #1: "I forget!" Lay it on your nightstand or on your
desk—or better yet, on the coffee table for everyone to see—so
that you'll be reminded that it's there.

Excuse #2: "I don't have time!" I get it. I do. But we all have five
minutes. Wake up five minutes earlier. Go to bed five minutes
later. And fill that time with the wisdom of God's Word.

Excuse #3: "The words are too hard, too boring." Find a Bible
translation that's written in a way that you enjoy, that is easier or
more interesting for you. There are even apps that will read it to you!

There really is a way to make His Word a part of every day. It's your armor. It's your truth. It is "a lamp for my feet and a light on my path" (Psalm 119:105).

Best of all, it is "inspired by God." And isn't that all you really need to know?

WITH THE SPIRIT WITHIN ME

Do you not know that you are a temple of God and that the Spirit of God dwells in you?—1 Corinthians 3:16 NASB

Read that verse again. Think about it.

The grandest cathedral with the highest ceilings, the most elaborate steeple, the largest auditorium *ain't got nothing on you*! On that day of Pentecost, when the Helper whom Jesus promised arrived, the Spirit of God came down and filled His people (Acts 2). That means, as unbelievable as it may seem, the Spirit of God dwells within you, within anyone who believes in Him.

No matter how beautiful, how big, or how fancy the church building, God wants to be right there, in your heart. He wants to be with His people, leading them, guiding them, and giving them strength. And when the world is against you, when fear or pain or sadness sets in, you can turn there, to that strength inside you.

As Paul told the young disciple Timothy, "God has not given us a spirit of fearfulness, but one of power, love, and sound judgment" (2 Timothy 1:7). Our God is a God of power, a God of love, and a God of sound judgment. The Holy Spirit living inside us gives us those qualities too.

This also means that when you feel that nudge to say hello, to offer a helping hand, to say a prayer for someone, it's probably that Spirit of love showing you the right direction. Use your brain, of course, but tune in and listen to that Spirit.

Finally, don't forget that you *are* a temple. Your body holds inside of it the most precious gift of the Holy Spirit. And because of that, your body has a lot of work to do in this world. Be good to it. Keep it clean and tidy. Respect it. Love it. It's not yours to mistreat or neglect. Your body is a temple of God.

WITH THE FAITHFUL BESIDE ME

If God is for us, who is against us?
—Romans 8:31

I hope that the words of Romans 8:31 make you feel the same way I do. I get chills when I hear them or even read them on the page. Those nine words make me feel safe, powerful, and loved. The verse reminds me, simply and powerfully, that God is for me. For *me*.

And with God cheering for me, fighting for me, loving me—and all His people—what is there really to fear? What is it that we, as His people, cannot overcome?

He has made us for each other. Together, you, me, all of us—we make up the "us" in that verse, the body of Christ here on this earth. Some of us are great leaders. Some of us will take instructions and go get the job done. Some of us are inspiring teachers. Some of us are good at sitting and holding someone's hand while that person talks. Some of us are so in tune with the Spirit of God that it's like we hear Him talking out loud.

But none of us, that I've seen, are *all* those things. None of us have *all* the gifts. Just like the human body, each part in the body of Christ performs a different function.

The mouth doesn't eat by itself. It gets a lot of help from the hands and the stomach. The brain won't work very well if the lungs stop moving air. And the whole thing shuts down if the brain stops working. When all the body parts are healthy, doing the job they were meant to do, the body does its best work.

In the same way, the body of Christ, with each body part doing its best work, can be a super-powerful thing. We can quite literally change the world. But what part are you? I bet you have a better idea now than before you started this book. And next year you'll know more about your role in the church than you do now.

But just keep seeking God, and He'll give you tasks for you to perform. Then you'll be playing your part.

When we serve Him, taking our place in the body of Christ, He is for us. Who could *ever* be against us?

WITH THE WORLD AROUND ME

"But take heart! I have overcome the world."
—John 16:33 NIV

Before Jesus was arrested, He told His disciples about what was coming. He told His disciples that they would grieve, but that their grief would turn to joy (John 16:20). He told them simple details. He told them things they didn't yet understand. But through it all, He was preparing them for trouble. Then He said, "I have told you these things, so that in me you may have peace. In this world you will have trouble. But take heart! I have overcome the world" (John 16:33 NIV).

Jesus never said it would all be rainbows and cupcakes. Jesus never promised a life of wealth and comfort. He told His disciples —and us—that there would be troubles in this world. But the overwhelming truth, the truth we need to always remember, is that Jesus has already overcome the world.

Before He hung on the cross, He had already overcome the world. But as He hung there helpless, it surely didn't look like it. In fact, the world may have called Him a criminal, a dead man, a liar, a crook. Lucky for us, Jesus's identity was not decided by the world and their opinions. Who Jesus was did not change because people sneered and laughed at Him. Instead of Jesus being changed by the world's views, Jesus took their point of view and turned it upside down.

An earthquake shook the land. The temple curtain tore in two. It became dark in the middle of the day. And the guard who had just been laughing at Jesus a minute before stood with his mouth hanging open and said, "Truly this was the Son of God!" (Matthew 27:54 NASB).

The most wonderful thing about our identity is this: it has very little to do with who we are and *everything* to do with who He is. And when we know that, we are fearless—comfortable and confident with telling others exactly who we are, showing them with our actions, declaring it with our love.

He is our God. We are His children. And in Him and through Him we too have already overcome the world.

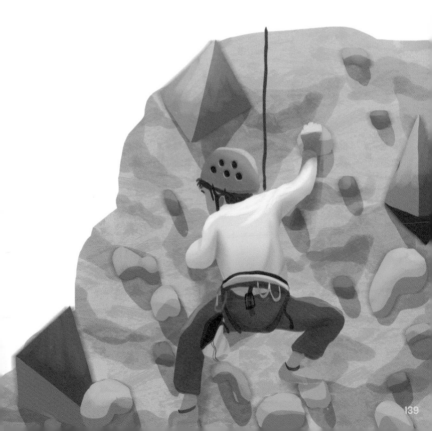

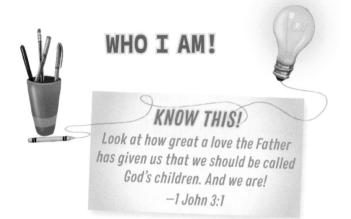

WHO I AM!

Like we did at the beginning of the book, we're going to take a look at who you are.

Name: _____

Age: _____ Grade: _____

_____

I know that *I AM UNIQUE* because _____

_____

_____

I know that *I AM HUMAN* because _____

_____

_____

I know that *I AM MADE NEW* because _____

_____

_____

I know that *I AM LOVED* because _____

_____

I know that *I AM A CHILD OF GOD* because _____

_____

I know that *I AM AN EXAMPLE* because _____

_____

I know that *I AM NOT ALONE* because _____

_____

I know that *I AM CALLED* because _____

_____

THE WONDERS OF YOU

The largest human organ is the . . .
skin. It protects the body from lots
and lots of harmful germs![10]

10. https://nutritionstudies.org/body-heals/

REMEMBER:

For in Christ all the fullness of the Deity lives in bodily form, and in Christ you have been brought to fullness.—Colossians 2:9–10 NIV

READ:

The story of David and Goliath (1 Samuel 17) isn't just about a boy defeating a giant. It's about a young man who is confident in God, in his identity as a child of God. When Goliath mocks God and His people, experienced warriors all run and hide from the Philistine giant. But when David hears the giant's insults, he can't believe that God's people are doing nothing. He marches right out there and battles that giant, knowing that the battle is the Lord's and the full strength of the Almighty God is within him.

THINK:

1. Look back at David's conversation with King Saul (1 Samuel 17:34–37). How had God prepared David to fight the giant?

2. Notice how David fought the giant. He didn't use the king's armor to protect him. What did he use?

3. What are some of the giants you face today?

4. David fought the giant using his skills, his gifts, and his faith. How has God uniquely prepared you to fight the giants before you?

DO:

Draw an outline of yourself. Now, draw or write the things that Christ fills you up with. How are you brought to fullness in Christ?

Always remember that "in Christ you have been brought to fullness" to help you face the challenges of this world. With your faith and your identity placed firmly in Christ, together you can defeat whatever giants may come your way.